SB1002

C000157090

THE WORLD'S GREAT HYMNS

50 FAVORITE HYMNS OF FAITH

Shawnee Press, Inc.

A Subsidiary of Music Sales Corporation
1221 17th Avenue South · Nashville, TN 37212

Visit Shawnee Press Online at www.shawneepress.com

A Mighty Fortress Is Our God

Martin Luther; translated by Frederick H. Hedge

Martin Luther

With power ♩ = 104

C   C/E   C   G   Em7   Am7   Dsus   D   G   Am7   Em7   F2   C2   Am

f

1. A might-y for-tress is___ our God, A bul-wark nev - er

(2. Did) we in our__ own strength_ con - fide, Our striv - ing would be

with pedal

F   Gsus   G   C   C/E   C   G   Em7

4

fail - ing; Our help - er He__ a -

los - ing, Were not the right__ man

Am7   Dsus   D   G   Am7   Em7   F2   C2   Am   F   Gsus   G   C   C/E

7

mid__ the flood Of mor - tal ills pre - vail - ing. For

on__ our side, The man of God's own choos - ing. Dost

Verse 3

And though this world, with devils filled,
Should threaten to undo us.
We will not fear, for God hath willed
His truth to triumph thru us.

The prince of darkness grim,
We tremble not for him—
His rage we can endure,
For lo, his doom is sure:
One little word shall fell him.

Verse 4

That word above all earthly powers,
No thanks to them, a bideth;
The Spirit and the gifts are ours
Thru Him who with us sideth.

Let goods and kindred go,
This mortal life also—
The body they may kill;
God's truth abideth still:
His kingdom is forever.

All Creatures of Our God and King

St. Francis of Assisi
Translated by William H. Draper

Geistlishe Kirchengesange

Verse 3

Thou flowing water, pure and clear,
Make music for thy Lord to hear,
Alleluia, Alleluia!

Thou fire so masterful and bright,
That givest man both warmth and light,
O praise Him, O praise Him,
Alleluia, alleluia, alleluia!

Verse 4

And all ye men of tender heart,
Forgiving others, take your part,
O sing ye, Alleluia!

Ye who long pain and sorrow bear,
Praise God and on Him cast your care,
O praise Him, O praise Him,
Alleluia, alleluia, alleluia!

Verse 5

Let all things their Creator bless,
And worship Him in humbleness,
O praise Him, Alleluia!

Praise, praise the Father, praise the Son,
And praise the Spirit, Three in One,
O praise Him, O praise Him,
Alleluia, alleluia, alleluia!

All Hail the Power of Jesus' Name

Edward Perronet; Adapted by John Rippon

Oliver Holden

Verse 4

Let every kindred, every tribe,
On this terestrial ball,
To Him all majesty ascribe,
And crown Him Lord of all;
To Him all majesty ascribe,
And crown Him Lord of all!

Verse 5

O that with yonder sacred throng
We at His feet may fall!
We'll join the everlasting song,
And crown Him Lord of all;
We'll join the everlasting song,
And crown Him Lord of all!

O for a Thousand Tongues

Charles Wesley

Carl G. Gläzer

Verse 3

He breaks the pow'r of cancelled sin,
He sets the prisoner free;
His blood can make the foulest clean;
His blood availed for me.

Verse 4

Hear Him, ye deaf; His praise, ye dumb,
Your loosened tongues employ;
Ye blind, behold your Savior come;
And leap, ye lame, for joy.

Verse 5

My gracious Master and my God,
Assist me to proclaim,
To spread thro' all the earth abroad,
The honors of Thy name.

Alleluia! Sing to Jesus

William C. Dix

Rowland H. Prichard

Verse 3

Alleluia! Bread of Heaven,
You on earth our food, and stay!
Alleluia! here the sinful
Flee to You from day to day;

Intercessor, Friend of sinners,
Earth's Redeemer, plead for me,
Where the songs of all the sinless
Sweep across the crystal sea.

Amazing Grace

John Newton; John P. Rees, stanza 5

**Traditional American melody from
Carrell and Clayton's *Virginia Harmony*, 1831**

Verse 3
>   The Lord has promised good to me,
>   His word my hope secures;
>   He will my shield and portion be
>   As long as life endures.

Verse 4
>   Thro' many dangers, toils, and snares
>   I have already come.
>   'Tis grace hath brought me safe thus far,
>   And grace will lead me home.

Verse 5
>   When we've been there ten thousand years,
>   Bright shining as the sun,
>   We've no less days to sing God's praise
>   Than when we'd first begun.

At Calvary

William R. Newell

Daniel B. Towner

With confidence and joy ♩ = 104

1. Years I spent in van - i - ty and pride,
2. By God's Word at last my sin I learned–

Car - ing not my Lord was cru - ci - fied, Know - ing not it was for
Then I trem - bled at the law I'd spurned, Till my guilt - y soul im-

me He died On Cal - va - ry.
plor - ing died turned To Cal - va - ry.

Verse 3
Now I've given to Jesus everything,
Now I gladly own Him as my king,
Now my raptured soul can only sing
Of Calvary.

Verse 4
O the love that drew salvation's plan!
O the grace that brought it down to man!
O the mighty gulf that God did span
At Calvary.

Blessed Assurance

Fanny J. Crosby

Phoebe P. Knapp

Verse 3

Perfect submission, all is at rest,
I in my Savior am happy and blest;
Watching and waiting, looking above,
Filled with His goodness, lost in His love.

Blessed Be the Name

William H. Clark; Ralph E. Hudson, Refrain

Verse 3

His Name shall be the Counselor,
The mighty Prince of Peace,
Of all earth's kingdoms Conqueror,
Whose reign shall never cease.

Come, Thou Fount of Every Blessing

Robert Robinson

Traditional American melody

Verse 3

O to grace how great a debtor
Daily I'm constrained to be!
Let Thy goodness, like a fetter,
Bind my wandering heart to Thee:

Prone to wander, Lord, I feel it,
Prone to leave the God I love;
Here's my heart, O take a seal it;
Seal if for They courts above.

Crown Him with Many Crowns

Matthew Bridges, stanzas 1, 2, 4
Godfrey Thring, stanza 3

George J. Elvey

Verse 3

Crown Him the Lord of life:
Who triumphed o'er the grave
Who rose victorious to the strife
For those He came to save.

His glories now we sing,
Who died and rose on high,
Who died eternal life to bring
And lives that death may die.

Verse 4

Crown Him the Lord of heav'n:
One with the Father known,
One with the Spirit thru Him giv'n
From yonder glorious throne.

To Thee be endless praise,
For Thou for us hast died;
Be Thou, O Lord, thru endless days
Adored and magnified.

Fairest Lord Jesus

Anonymous German Hymn

Schlesische Volkslieder, **1842**

Verse 3

Fair is the sunshine, Fairer still the moonlight,
And all the twinkling starry host:
Jesus shines brighter, Jesus shines purer
Than all the angels heaven can boast.

Verse 4

Beautiful Savior! Lord of the nations!
Son of God and Son of Man!
Glory and honor, Praise, adoration,
Now and forevermore be Thine!

For the Beauty of the Earth

Folliott S. Pierpoint, altered

Conrad Kocher

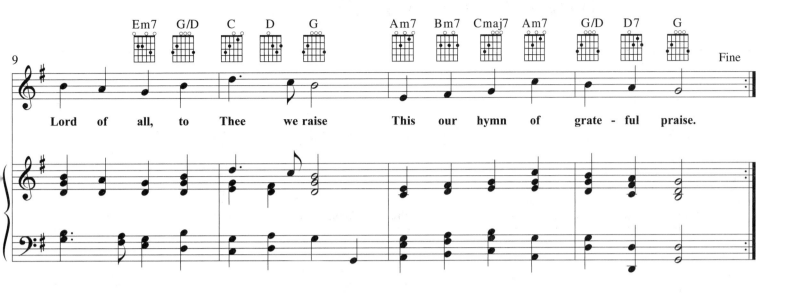

Lord of all, to Thee we raise This our hymn of grate - ful praise.

Fine

Verse 3

For the joy of human love,
Brother, sister, parent, child;
Friends on earth and friends above;
For all gentle thoughts and mild:

Lord of all, to Thee we raise
This our hymn of grateful praise.

Verse 4

For Thy Church taht evermore
Lifteth holy hands above,
Offering up on every shore
Her pure sacrifice of love:

Lord of all, to Thee we raise
This our hymn of grateful praise.

Verse 5

For Thyself, best gift divine,
To our race so freely given;
For that great, great love of Thine,
Peace on earth and joy in heaven:

Lord of all, to Thee we raise
This our hymn of grateful praise.

Glorious Things of Thee Are Spoken

John Newton

Franz Joseph Haydn

Verse 3

Round each habitation hovering,
See the cloud and fire appear
For a glory and a covering,
Showing that the Lord is near!

Thus deriving from their banner
Light by night and shade by day,
Safe they feed upon the manna
Which He gives them when they pray.

Guide Me, O Thou Great Jehovah

William Williams

John Hughes

Verse 3

When I tread the verge of Jordan,
Bid y anxious fears subside;
Bear me thro' the swelling current,
Land me safe on Cannan's side;

Songs of praises, songs of praises
I will ever give to Thee,
I will ever give to Thee.

Higher Ground

Johnson Oatman, Jr.

Charles H. Gabriel

Verse 4
I want to scale the utmost height
And catch a gleam of glory bright;
But still I'll pray till heav'n I've found,
"Lord, lead me on to higher ground."

Verse 3
I want to live above the world,
Tho Satan's darts at me are hurled;
For faith has caught the joyful sound,
The song of saints on higher ground.

Holy, Holy, Holy

Reginald Heber

John B. Dykes

Verse 3

Holy, holy, holy! though the darkness hide Thee,
Though the eye of sinful man Thy glory may not see;
Only Thou art holy– there is none beside Thee,
Perfect in pow'r in love and purity.

Verse 4

Holy, holy, holy! Lord God Almighty!
All Thy works shall praise Thy name in earth and sky and sea;
Holy, holy, holy! merciful and mighty!
God in three Persons, blessed Trinity!

How Firm a Foundation

Rippon's *Selection of Hymns*, 1787

Traditional American melody
Caldwell's Union Harmony, 1837

Verse 3
    "When through fiery trials thy pathway shall lie,
    My grace, all sufficient, shall be thy supply:
    The flame shall not hurt thee; I only design
    Thy dross to consume and they gold to refine.

Verse 4
    "The soul that on Jesus hath learned for repose
    I will not, I will not desert to its foes;
    That soul, though all hell should endeavor to shake,
    I'll never, no, never, no, never forsake!"

I Know Whom I Have Believed

Daniel W. Whittle

James McGranahan

Verse 3
I know not how the Spirit moves,
Convincing men of sin,
Revealing Jesus through the Word,
Creating faith in Him.

Verse 4
I know not when my Lord may come,
At night or noonday fair,
Nor if I'll walk the vale with Him,
Or "meet Him in the air."

I Love to Tell the Story

A. Catherine Hankey

William G. Fischer

Verse 3
I love to tell the story, for those who know it best
Seem hungering and thristing to hear it like the rest;
And when in scenes of glory, I sing the new, new song,
'Twill be the old, old story that I have loved so long.

I Sing the Mighty Power of God

Isaac Watts, altered

From *Gesangbuch der Herzogl*, Württemberg, 1784

Verse 3

There's not a plant or flow'r below,
But makes Thy glories known;
And clouds arise, and tempests blow,
By order from Thy throne;

While all that borrows life from Thee
Is ever in Thy care,
And ev'rywhere that man can be,
Thou, God, art present there.

I Will Sing of the Mercies

Based on Psalm 89:1

James H. Fillmore

Immortal, Invisible

Walter Chalmers Smith

Traditional Welsh Hymn melody

1. Im - mor - tal, in - vis - i - ble, God on - ly wise, In light in - ac - ces - i - ble hid from our eyes, Most bless - ed, most glo - rious, the An - cient of

(2. Un) - rest - ing, un - hast - ing, and si - lent as light, Nor want - ing, nor wast - ing, Thou rul - est in might; Thy jus - tice, like moun - tains, high soar - ing a -

with pedal

Verse 3

> To all, life Thou givest– to both great and small,
> In all life Thou livest– the true life of all;
> We blossom and flourish as leaves on the tree,
> And wither and perish– but naught changeth Thee.

Verse 4

> Great Father of glory, pure Father of light,
> Thine angels adore Thee, all veiling their sight;
> All praise we would render– O help us to see
> 'Tis only the splendor of light hideth Thee!

It Is Well with My Soul

Horatio G. Spafford

Philip P. Bliss

With warmth ♩ = 100

1. When peace like a riv - er at - tend - eth my
(2. Though) Sa - tan should buf - fet, tho' tri - als should

with pedal

way, When sor - rows like sea bil - lows roll; What -
come, Let this blest as - sur - ance con - trol, That

ev - er my lot, Thou hast taught me to say, "It is
Christ has re - gard - ed my help - less es - tate, And hath

Verse 3

My sin– O, the bliss of this glorious thought,
My sin– not in part but the whole,
Is nailed to the cross and I bear it no more,
Praise the Lord, praise the Lord, O my soul!

Verse 4

And, Lord, haste the day when the faith shall be sight,
The couds be rolled back as a scroll,
The trump shall resound and the Lord shall descend,
"Even so–" it is well with my soul.

Jesus Paid It All

Elvina M. Hall

John T. Grape

Verse 3

    For nothing good have I
    Whereby Thy grace to claim–
    I'll wash my garments white
    In the blood of Calv'ry's Lamb.

Verse 4

    And when before the throne
    I stand in Him complete,
    "Jesus died my soul to save,"
    My lips shall still repeat.

Joyful, Joyful, We Adore Thee

52

Henry van Dyke

Ludwig van Beethoven
Melody from Ninth Symphony

Verse 3

Thou art giving and forgiving,
Ever blessing, ever blest,
Wellspring of the joy of living,
Ocean depth of happy rest!

Thou our Father, Christ our brother—
All who live in love are Thine;
Teach us how to love each other,
Lift us to the joy divine.

Verse 4

Mortals, join the happy chorus
Which the morning stars began;
Father love is reigning o'er us,
Brother love binds man to man.

Ever singing, march we onward,
Victors in the midst of strife,
Joyful music leads us sunward
In the triumph song of life.

Just as I Am

Charlotte Elliott

William B. Bradbury

Not too slow ♩ = 104

N.C. F F/A C7 F2 F

mf

1. Just___ as I am,___ with - out___ one plea But
(2. Just)___ as I am,___ and wait - ing not To

with pedal

C/E Dm7 C7 Bb/F C/E F2 F Bb/C

that___ Thy blood was shed for me, And___
rid___ my soul of one dark blot, To___

F F/E Dm7 F/C Bb Bb/A Gm7 3fr. C7

that Thou bidd'st___ me come to Thee,___ O
Thee whose blood___ can cleanse each spot,___ O

Verse 3

       Just as I am, tho' tossed about
       With many a conflict, many a doubt,
       Fightings and fears within, without,
       O Lamb of God, I come! I come!

Verse 4

       Just as I am, poor, wretched, blind,
       Sight, riches, healing of the mind,
       Yea, all I need in Thee to find,
       O Lamb of God, I come! I come!

Lead On, O King Eternal

Earnest W. Shurtleff

Henry T. Smart

Verse 3

Lead on, O King Eternal,
We follow, not with fears;
For gladness breaks like morning
Where'er Your face appears;

Your cross is lifted o'er us;
We journey in its light:
The crown awaits the conquest;
Lead on, O God of might.

Leaning on the Everlasting Arms

Elisha A. Hoffman

Anthony J. Showalter

Verse 3

What have I to dread, what have I to fear,
Leaning on the everlasting arms?
I have blessed peace with my Lord so near,
Leaning on the everlasting arms.

My Faith Looks Up to Thee

Ray Palmer

Lowell Mason

Verse 3

    While life's dark maze I tread
    And griefs around me spread,
    Be Thou my guide;

    Bid darkness turn to day,
    Wipe sorrow's tears away,
    Nor let me ever stray
    From Thee aside.

Verse 4

    When ends life's passing dream,
    When death's cold, threatening stream
    Shall o'er me roll,

    Blest Savior, then, in love,
    Fear and distrust remove;
    O lift me safe above,
    A ransomed soul!

My Jesus, I Love Thee

William R. Featherstone

Adoniram J. Gordon

Verse 3

I'll love Thee in life; I will love Thee in death
And praise Thee as long as Thou lendest me breath;
And say when the death-dew lies cold on my brow,
"If ever I loved Thee, my Jesus, 'tis now."

Verse 4

In mansions of glory and endless delight,
I'll ever adore Thee in heaven so bright.
I'll sing with the glittering crown on my brow,
"If ever I loved Thee, my Jesus, 'tis now."

Near to the Heart of God

Cleland B. McAfee

Cleland B. McAfee

Verse 3
There is a place of full release
Near to the heart of God,
A place where all is joy and peace,
Near to the heart of God.

Nothing but the Blood of Jesus

Robert Lowry

Robert Lowry

Verse 3
Nothing can for sin atone,
Nothing but the blood of Jesus;
Naught of good that I have done,
Nothing but the blood of Jesus.

Verse 4
This is all my hope and peace,
Nothing but the blood of Jesus;
This is all my righteousness,
Nothing but the blood of Jesus.

Redeemed

Fanny J. Crosby

William J. Kirkpatrick

Verse 3

I think of by blessed Redeemer,
I think of Him all the day long;
I sing, for I cannot be silent;
His love is the theme of my song.

Verse 4

I know I shall see in His beauty
The King in whose law I delight;
Who lovingly guardeth my footsteps,
And giveth me songs in the night.

Rejoice, the Lord Is King

Charles Wesley

John Darwall

Verse 3
His kingdom cannot fail,
He rules o'er earth and heav'n;
The keys of death and hell
Are to our Jesus giv'n.

Verse 4
Rejoice in glorious hope!
Our Lord the Judge shall come
And take His servants up
To their eternal home:

Rock of Ages

Augustus M. Toplady

Thomas Hastings

Verse 3
>   Nothing in my hand I bring,
>   Simply to Thy cross I cling;
>   Naked, come to Thee for dress,
>   Helpless, look to Thee for grace;
>   Foul, I to the fountain fly,
>   Wash me, Savior, or I die!

Verse 4
>   While I draw this fleeting breath,
>   When my eyes shall close in death,
>   When I soar to worlds unknown,
>   See Thee on Thy judgment throne,
>   Rock of Ages, cleft for me,
>   Let me hide myself in Thee.

Savior, Like a Shepherd Lead Us

Hymns for the Young, 1836

William B. Bradbury

Verse 3

Thou hast promised to receive us,
Poor and sinful though we be;
Thou hast mercy to relieve us,
Grace to cleanse, and pow'r to free:

Blessed Jesus, blessed Jesus,
Early let us turn to Thee;
Blessed Jesus, blessed Jesus,
Early let us turn to Thee.

Verse 4

Early let us seek Thy favor;
Early let us do Thy will;
Blessed Lord and only Savior,
With Thy love our bossoms fill:

Blessed Jesus, blessed Jesus,
Thou hast loved us, love us still;
Blessed Jesus, blessed Jesus,
Thou hast loved us, love us still.

Softly and Tenderly

Will L. Thompson   **Will L. Thompson**

Tenderly, not too slow ♩ = 110

1. Soft - ly and ten - der - ly Je - sus is call - ing,
2. Why should we tar - ry when Je - sus is plead - ing,

with pedal

Call - ing for you and for me.
Plead - ing for you and for me?

See, on the por - tals He's wait - ing and watch - ing,
Why should we lin - ger and heed not His mer - cies,

Verse 3

Time is now fleeting; the moments are passing,
Passing from you and from me.
Shadows are gathering, death's night is coming,
Coming for you and for me.

Verse 4

O for the wonderful love He has promised,
Promised for you and for me!
Though we have sinned, He has mercy and pardon,
Pardon for you and for me.

Standing on the Promises

R. Kelso Carter

R. Kelso Carter

With a bounce ♩ = 108

1. Stand - ing on the prom - is - es of Christ my King,
2. Stand - ing on the prom - is - es that can - not fail,

Thro' e - ter - nal a - ges let His prais - es ring;
When the howl - ing storms of doubt and fear as - sail,

Glo - ry in the high - est, I will shout and sing,
By the liv - ing Word of God I shall pre - vail,

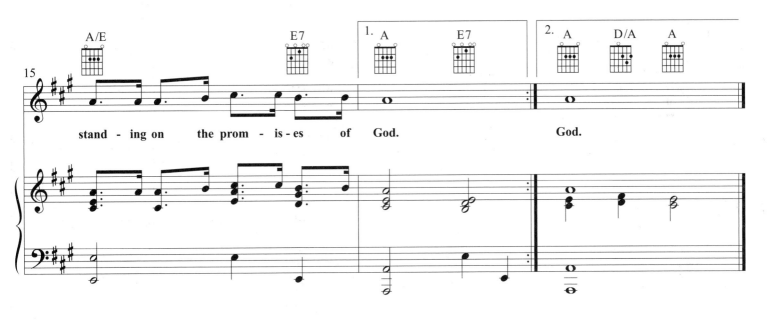

stand - ing on   the prom - is - es   of   God.   God.

Verse 3

      Standing on the promises of Christ the Lord,
      Bound to Him eternally by love's strong cord,
      Overcoming daily with the Spirit's sword,
      Standing on the promises of God.

Verse 4

      Standing on the promises I cannot fail,
      List'ning every moment to the Spirit's call,
      Resting in my Savior as my all in all,
      Standing on the promises of God.

Stand Up, Stand Up for Jesus

George Duffield, Jr.

George J. Webb

Verse 3

Stand up, stand up for Jesus,
Stand in His strength alone;
The arm of flesh will fail you–
Ye dare not trust your own;

Put on the gospel armor,
Each piece put on with prayer;
Where duty calls, or danger,
Be never wanting there.

Verse 4

Stand up, stand up for Jesus,
The strife will not be long;
This day the noise of battle,
The next, the victor's song;

To him who overcometh
A crown of life shall be;
He with the King of glory
Shall reign eternally.

Sweet Hour of Prayer

William W. Walford

William B. Bradbury

Take My Life and Let It Be

Frances R. Havergal

Henry A. C. Malan

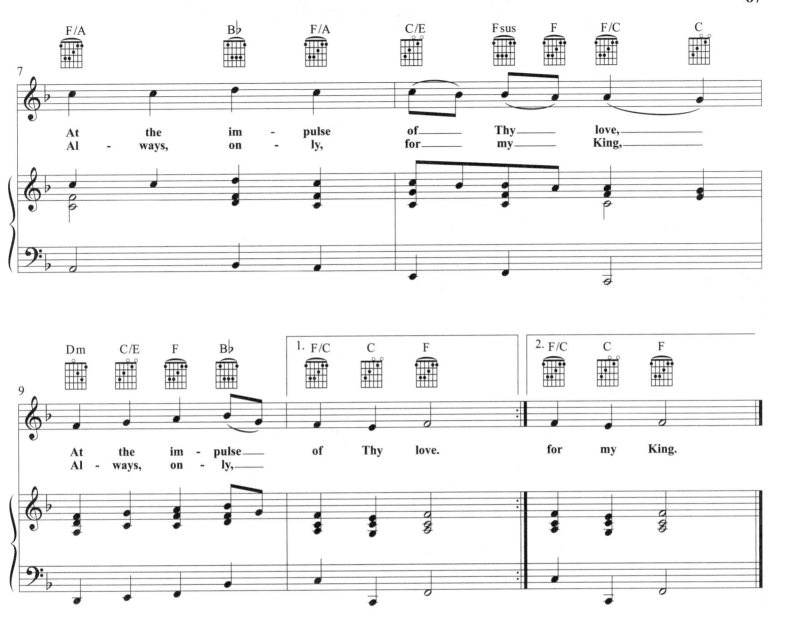

Verse 3
    Take my silver and my gold,
    Not a mite would I withhold;
    Take my moments and my days,
    Let them flow in ceaseless praise,
    Let them flow in ceaseless praise.

Verse 4
    Take my will and make it Thine,
    It shall be no longer mine;
    Take my heart and, it is Thine own,
    It shall be Thy royal throne,
    It shall be Thy royal throne.

The Solid Rock

Edward Mote

William B. Bradbury

Verse 3

His oath, His covenant, His blood
Support me in the whelming flood;
When all around my soul gives way,
He then is all my hope and stay.

Verse 4

When He shall come with trumpet sound,
O may I then in Him be found;
Dressed in His righteousness alone,
Faultless to stand before the throne.

There Is Power in the Blood

Lewis E. Jones

Lewis E. Jones

Verse 3
> Would you be whiter, much whiter than snow?
> There's pow'r in the blood, pow'r in the blood;
> Sin-stains are lost in its life-giving flow;
> There's wonderful pow'r in the blood.

Verse 4
> Would you do service for Jesus, your King?
> There's pow'r in the blood, pow'r in the blood;
> Would you live daily His praises to sing?
> There's wonderful pow'r in the blood.

'Tis So Sweet to Trust in Jesus

Louisa M. R. Stead

William J. Kirkpatrick

Verse 3

Yes, 'tis sweet to trust in Jesus,
Just from sin and self to cease,
Just from Jesus simply taking
Life and rest and joy and peace.

Verse 4

I'm so glad I learned to trust Him,
Precious Jesus, Savior, Friend;
And I know that He is with me,
Will be with me to the end.

We Gather Together

Netherlands Folk hymn
Translated by Theodore Baker

Netherlands Folk song

Flowing, in one ♩ = 108

1. We gath - er to - geth - er to
(2. Be) - side us to guide us, to our

with pedal

ask the Lord's bless - ing; He chas - tens and
God with us join - ing, Or - dain - ing, main -

has - tens His will to make known; The
tain - ing His king - dom di - vine; The So

Verse 3
We all do extol Thee, Thou Leader triumphant,
And pray that Thou still our Defender wilt be.
Let Thy congregation escape tribulation:
Thy name be ever praised! O Lord, make us free!

We're Marching to Zion

Isaac Watts; Robert Lowry, Refrain

Robert Lowry

Verse 3
The hill of Zion yields
A thousand sacred sweets
Before we reach the heavenly fields,
Before we reach the heavenly fields
Or walk the golden streets,
Or walk the golden streets.

Verse 4
Then let our songs abound,
And every tear be dry.
We're marching through Immanuel's ground,
We're marching through Immanuel's ground
To fairer worlds on high,
To fairer worlds on high.

When I Survey the Wondrous Cross

Isaac Watts

Based on a Gregorian Chant

1. When I sur- vey the won- drous cross
2. For- bid it, Lord, that I should boast,

On which the Prince of glo - ry died,
Save in the death of Christ, my God;

My rich- est gain I count as loss,
All the vain things that charm me most—

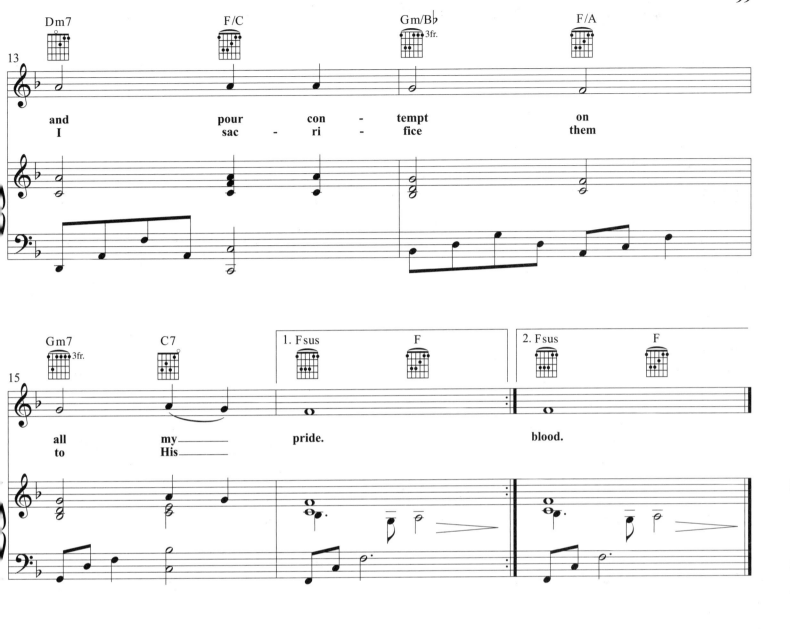

Verse 3
    See, from His head, His hands, His feet,
    Sorrow and love flow mingled down;
    Did e'er such love and sorrow meet,
    Or thorns compose so rich a crown?

Verse 4
    Were the whole realm of nature mine,
    That were a present far too small:
    Love so amazing, so divine,
    Demands my soul, my life, my all.

Whiter than Snow

James Nicholson

William G. Fischer

1. Lord Je - sus, I long to be per - fect - ly whole; I
(2. Lord) Je - sus, look down from Your throne in the skies I And

want Thee for - ev - er to live in my soul. Break
help me to make a com - plete sac - ri - fice. I

down ev - 'ry i - dol, cast out ev - 'ry foe, Now
give up my - self and what - ev - er I know, Now

101

Verse 3
Lord Jesus, for this I most humbly entreat;
I wait, blessed Lord, at Thy crucified feet.
By faith, for my cleansing I see Your blood flow.
Now wash me and I shall be whiter than snow.

Verse 4
Lord Jesus, before You I patiently wait;
Come now and within me a new heart create.
To those who have sought You, You never said, "No."
Now wash me and I shall be whiter than snow.

To God Be the Glory

Fanny J. Crosby

William H. Doane

Verse 3

Great things He hath taught us, great things He hath done,
And great our rejoicing through Jesus the Son;
But purer and higher and greater will be
Our wonder, our transport, when Jesus we see.